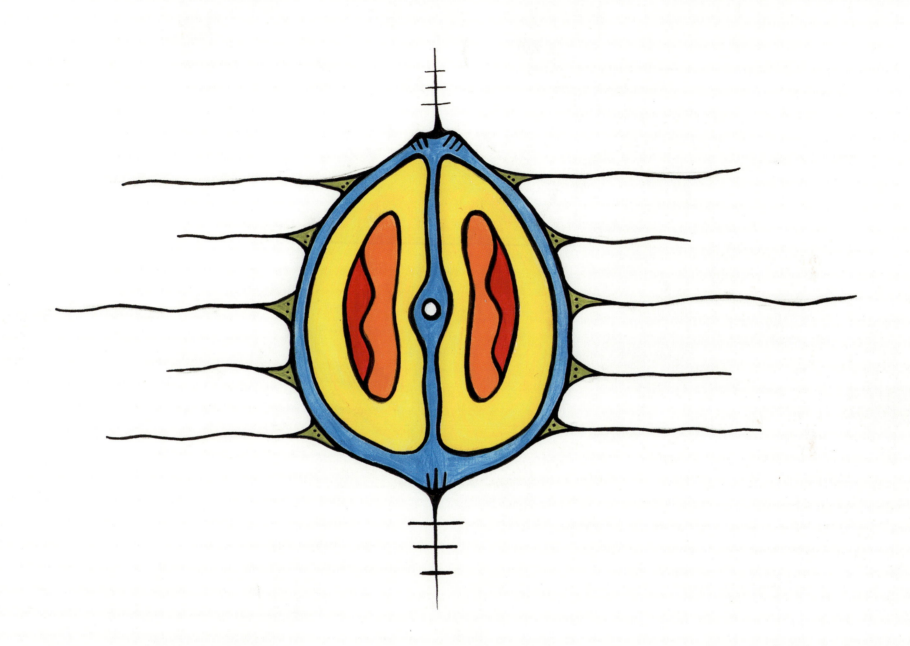

Text, excluding Illustrator's Note, copyright © 2025 by Karen Krossing
Illustrations and text for Illustrator's Note copyright © 2025 by Cathie Jamieson

All rights reserved. No part of this publication may be reproduced, stored in a retrieval system or transmitted, in any form or by any means, without the prior written consent of the publisher or a license from The Canadian Copyright Licensing Agency (Access Copyright). For an Access Copyright license, visit www.accesscopyright.ca or call toll free to 1-800-893-5777.

Published in 2025 by Groundwood Books / House of Anansi Press
groundwoodbooks.com

We gratefully acknowledge for their financial support of our publishing program the Canada Council for the Arts, the Ontario Arts Council and the Government of Canada.

Canada Council for the Arts / Conseil des Arts du Canada

ONTARIO ARTS COUNCIL
CONSEIL DES ARTS DE L'ONTARIO
an Ontario government agency
un organisme du gouvernement de l'Ontario

With the participation of the Government of Canada
Avec la participation du gouvernement du Canada | Canadä

The author acknowledges the support of the Ontario Arts Council during the writing of this book.

Library and Archives Canada Cataloguing in Publication
Title: My street remembers / written by Karen Krossing ; illustrated by Cathie Jamieson.
Names: Krossing, Karen, author. | Jamieson, Cathie, illustrator.
Description: Series statement: Better paths ; book 1
Identifiers: Canadiana (print) 20240528751 | Canadiana (ebook) 20240531035 | ISBN 9781773066356 (hardcover) | ISBN 9781773066363 (EPUB) |
Subjects: LCSH: Indigenous peoples—Canada—History—Juvenile literature. | LCSH: Indigenous peoples—North America—History—Juvenile literature. | LCSH: Canada—History—Juvenile literature. | LCSH: United States—History—Juvenile literature. | LCSH: Canada—Ethnic relations—History—Juvenile literature. | LCSH: United States—Ethnic relations—History—Juvenile literature. | LCGFT: Picture books.
Classification: LCC E77.4 .K76 2025 | DDC j971.004/97—dc23

The illustrations were created in acrylics.
Edited by Karen Li
Designed by Michael Solomon
Printed and bound in South Korea

MIX
Paper | Supporting responsible forestry
FSC® C140526

MY STREET

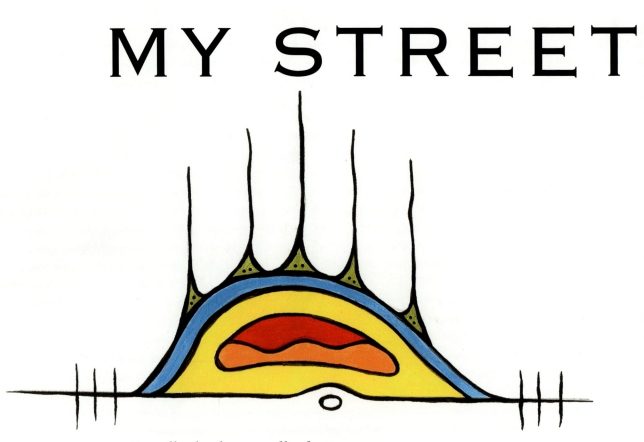

For all who have walked my street —
yesterday, today and tomorrow. — KK

To the inner child in each of us, to know
we can explore and play within the place
we call home. — CJ

REMEMBERS

WRITTEN BY Karen Krossing
ILLUSTRATED BY Cathie Jamieson

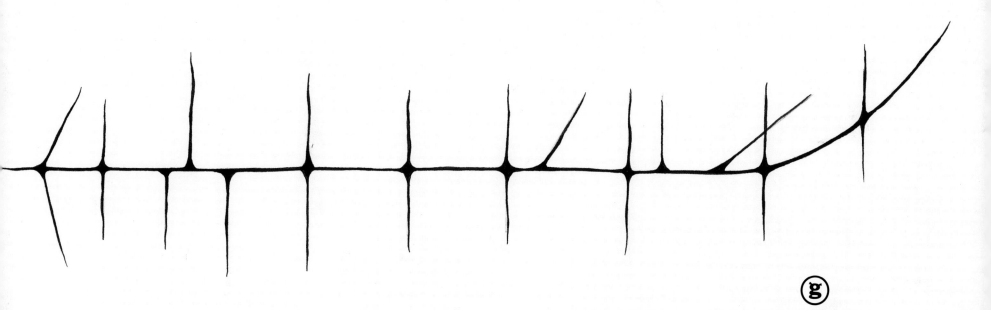

GROUNDWOOD BOOKS
HOUSE OF ANANSI PRESS
TORONTO / BERKELEY

My street remembers
everyone who travels our land now

and everyone who once did.

Over 14,000 years ago

From the long-ago mammoths and mastodons who roamed this ice-covered land,

About 1,000 Years Ago

About 500 Years Ago

It remembers how their descendants stepped in harmony with this land for thousands of years.

1600s

My street remembers
the hard-heeled boots
of the Europeans
who arrived later,

how they dreamed of routes
to faraway lands,
traded and traveled,
and brought wagon-loads of settlers
in their wake.

Together, they viewed this land as a dish eaten with just one spoon.

1787

My street remembers a meeting —
where the Mississauga People brought witnesses for a talk
on how to share the use of their Territory,

while the British brought gifts as an offer to buy it and a blank deed that was never signed.

It remembers the settlers who built their homes
in Mississauga Territory,
tilled the soil
and widened my street
to fit their carts and carriages.

My street will never forget the conflicts, suffering and people who were turned away.

My street remembers when we moved here as babies, unaware of those who had come before.

It remembers the tread of your first steps
and my first skinned knee.

My street remembers all of us on our land now
and each one who has passed before.
My street welcomes those to come.

Together, we find ways to heal past wrongs and share the journey forward.

What does your street remember?

A Brief History of a Street

A street is more than a place on a map. It's a story of our collective relationship with the land. A story shaped by glaciers and shifting landforms. A story inhabited by creatures who created paths, later followed by First (or Indigenous) Peoples. A story of many languages, journeys, meals shared, homes built and destroyed, sacred ceremonies and tragedies that could have been avoided. Each street holds a story to tell.

The street in this book is based on Danforth Avenue, a road on the land that is currently called Toronto, or Tkaranto in Kanien'kéha (gah-NYEN-geh-hah), meaning "trees in the water." The story of this street is one among many stories of many streets around the world. Here's a brief history of Danforth Avenue:

- Indigenous Peoples have lived in this area since time immemorial. They include the Wendat, the Haudenosaunee (ho-deh-no-SHAW-nee), the Anishinabeg (uh-NISH-ih-NAH-beg) and the Mississaugas (who are part of the Anishinabeg).

- When Europeans arrived in what is now known as North America, they were looking for a new trade route between Europe and Asia. The Frenchman Étienne Brûlé (eh-TYEN bru-LEH) arrived in Mississauga Territory by boat with Wendat scouts in 1615. He is thought to have been the first European in the area. Europeans brought goods to trade, as well as deadly new diseases.

- In 1640, the Haudenosaunee began a series of conflicts, known as the Beaver Wars, against other Indigenous Peoples in the region. They sought to increase their Territory and access to animals like beavers to trade their pelts with the French.

- Danforth Avenue is within Dish with One Spoon Territory. This was a peace agreement among Indigenous Peoples in the region, finalized in 1701, that defined Territories and how resources such as hunting grounds might be shared with permission. This treaty has been falsely portrayed in land acknowledgment statements as an agreement to nurture the environment for the mutual benefit of all, blurring the rights of Indigenous Peoples.

- In 1787, the British government, who valued written promises, met with three Mississauga leaders, who brought many witnesses for a verbal promise. The British offered to buy land with a gift, including 24 brass kettles, 120 mirrors, 24 laced hats and 160 blankets, as well as a deed that didn't describe the land to be purchased. Since the Mississauga People didn't buy or sell land, they viewed treaties as a way to share the use of their Territory. Unable to read English, the Mississauga leaders signed their marks on separate pieces of paper. The British later attached these to the blank deed, which was not a legal treaty.

- The British went on to build settlements in Mississauga Territory, displacing those who lived there. Eventually, the British realized they would need a treaty for the land they were occupying without consent. In 1805, they convinced the Mississaugas to sign the Toronto Purchase. It gave the Mississaugas only 10 shillings (about three days' wages) and local fishing rights for land that was bigger than 640,000 hockey rinks (about 250,800 acres). The British did not properly inform the Mississauga People about what they were agreeing to.

- Government laws limited where the Indigenous Peoples could go, banned their languages and celebrations, and forced their children into residential schools far from their families and communities. All these policies were acts of cultural genocide. Meanwhile, settlers continued to colonize the land that became Danforth Avenue.

- During the War of 1812, American forces invaded during the Battle of York on April 27, 1813. The war ended in 1815 with no change in ownership.

- Nineteenth-century Toronto was mostly White British Protestants. Other cultural groups faced bias and unfair laws. Africans who came to this land against their will endured oppression and racism, as have their descendants. Many leaders in the community enslaved Black people, and the last recorded sale of a person in Upper Canada dates from 1824. Among others, Irish Catholic newcomers were not welcomed, and clashes against them continued until after World War II.

- In 1851, Danforth Avenue was named after Asa Danforth, the American contractor first commissioned to build the route east of Toronto. This street became part of the country of Canada when it was formed in 1867. It was paved by 1915.

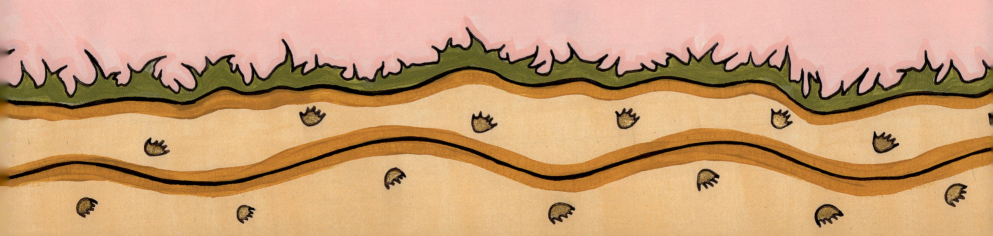

- Many newcomers arrived after World Wars I and II. Italian and Greek immigrants made it known as Greektown, and successive and diverse communities have continued to arrive and settle on this street.

- In 2010, the Canadian government paid the Mississauga People $145 million as a land claim settlement. Land claims are typically resolved with a payment of money, which doesn't repair the continued loss of independence and opportunity.

- With the release of the 2015 Truth and Reconciliation Report, the Canadian government committed to 94 calls to action to redress the legacy of residential schools and advance the process of reconciliation. By the first publication of this book, Indigenous Watchdog reported that only 14 calls to action had been completed with 15 yet to be started.

- In addition to its place within the Traditional Territory of the Wendat, Haudenosaunee and Anishinabeg, as well as the Treaty Lands and Territory of the Mississaugas of the Credit, Danforth Avenue is also home to many other First Nations, Inuit and the Métis.

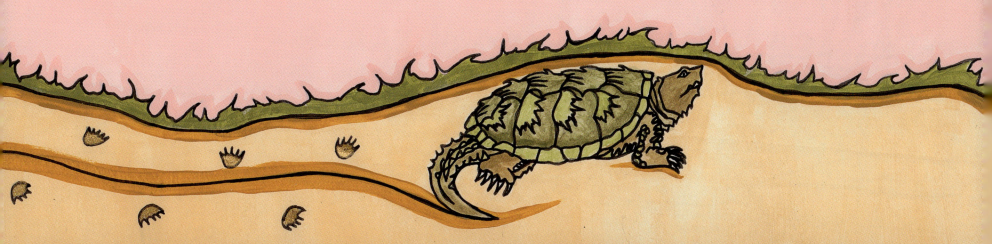

Illustrator's Note

These illustrations are a reminder that we do not make place, but place makes us. The places we call home — where we live and grow — will always have an impact on our lives. Place will always shape who we become in the future. Place will always nourish and provide for everyone who comes to stay and explore. All that is asked for in return is unconditional respect and kindness.

— CJ

Author's Note

The street in this book, now known as Danforth Avenue, is based on the one in Toronto where I live. The words within this book share my story of acknowledging past and present injustices, working to heal wounds and celebrating the joys of this land.

My ancestors came from Scotland, and I'm descended from White settlers. They benefitted from treaties and laws that harmed Indigenous Peoples, and I've had advantages because of my background. Researching, writing and collaborating on this book was an act of reconciliation for me. A way to reach out a hand to the Indigenous Peoples as traditional inhabitants of this land and community partners of yesterday, today and tomorrow.

The land that became our streets settles on us as we settle on it. It is a witness to what we've done right and wrong. Like us and our understanding of history, it continues to change, hopefully for the better.

— KK

Sources for Street Stories

The story of a street takes many lifetimes to tell. What story does your street tell? We've created a guide on how to learn about it, which you can find at groundwoodbooks.com.

To get a full picture, it's best to listen to a variety of people and consult a variety of resources. While creating this book, we consulted with people of Indigenous heritage to listen, seek advice and learn. In particular, we acknowledge the wisdom and support of Darin P. Wybenga, Traditional Knowledge and Land Use Coordinator of the Mississaugas of the Credit First Nation, and Dr. Mary Ann Corbiere, Associate Professor Emerita, University of Sudbury. Here are some of the resources we used for this book:

"About NCTR." *National Centre for Truth and Reconciliation*. University of Manitoba, 2022. Online.

Bunch, Adam. *The Toronto Book of the Dead*. Toronto: Dundurn Press, 2017.

Gannon, Megan I. "The Knotty Question of When Humans Made the Americas Home." *SAPIENS*, 4 Sept. 2019. Online.

Jacobs, Dean M. and Victor P. Lytwyn. "Naagan ge bezhig emkwaan: A Dish with One Spoon Reconsidered." *Ontario History*, vol. 112, no. 2, 2020, pp. 191–210.

Jurgens, Olga. "Étienne Brûlé." *Dictionary of Canadian Biography*, vol. 1. University of Toronto/Université Laval, 2015. Online.

Mackay, Claire. *The Toronto Story* (Johnny Wales, Illus.). Toronto: Annick Press, 2002.

"Map." *Whose Land*. BOLD Realities, TakingITGlobal and Canadian Roots Exchange. Online.

Mississaugas of the New Credit First Nation. *Toronto Purchase Specific Claim: Arriving at an Agreement*. Hagersville: Mississaugas of the New Credit First Nation. Online.

Myrvold, Barbara. *Historical Walking Tour of the Danforth*. Toronto: Toronto Public Library Board, 1992.

Myrvold, Barbara. *The Danforth in Pictures*. Toronto: Toronto Public Library Board, 1979.

"Native Land Digital." *Native-Land.ca*. Native Land Digital, 2024. Online.

Praxis Research Associates. *The History of the Mississaugas of the New Credit First Nation*. Hagersville: Mississaugas of the New Credit First Nation. Online.

Rogers, Edward S. and Donald B. Smith (editors). *Aboriginal Ontario: Historical Perspectives on the First Nations*. Toronto: Dundurn Press, 1994.

Sellers, Daniel. "Prehistoric Toronto: The Terrain of Our City Through the Ages" (Chloe Cushman, Illus.) *Torontoist*. Wayback Machine Internet Archive, 12 Apr. 2012. Online.

"Storied Toronto." *Toronto Historical Association*. Toronto Historical Association, 2020. Online.

"Welcome to the Moccasin Identifier." *The Moccasin Identifier*. The Moccasin Identifier, 2024. Online.

Wise, Leonard and Allan Gould. *Toronto Street Names: An Illustrated Guide to Their Origins*. Toronto: Firefly Books, 2011.

Wybenga, Darin P. and Kaytee Dalton. *Mississaugas of the New Credit First Nation*. Hagersville: Mississaugas of the New Credit First Nation, 2018. Online.